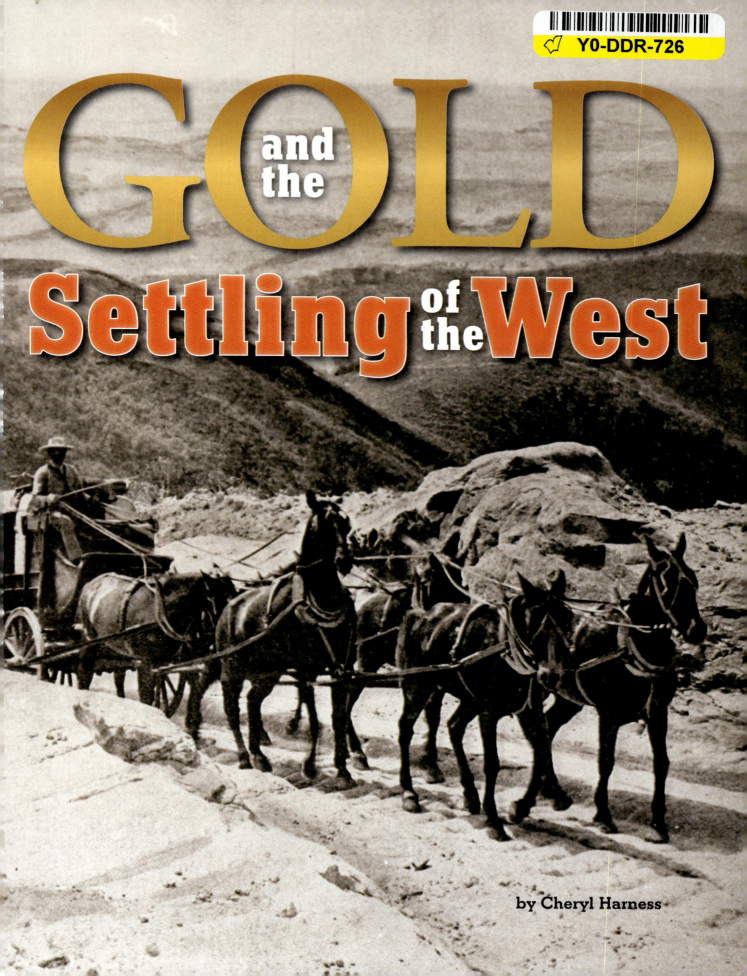

GOLD
and the
Settling of the West

by Cheryl Harness

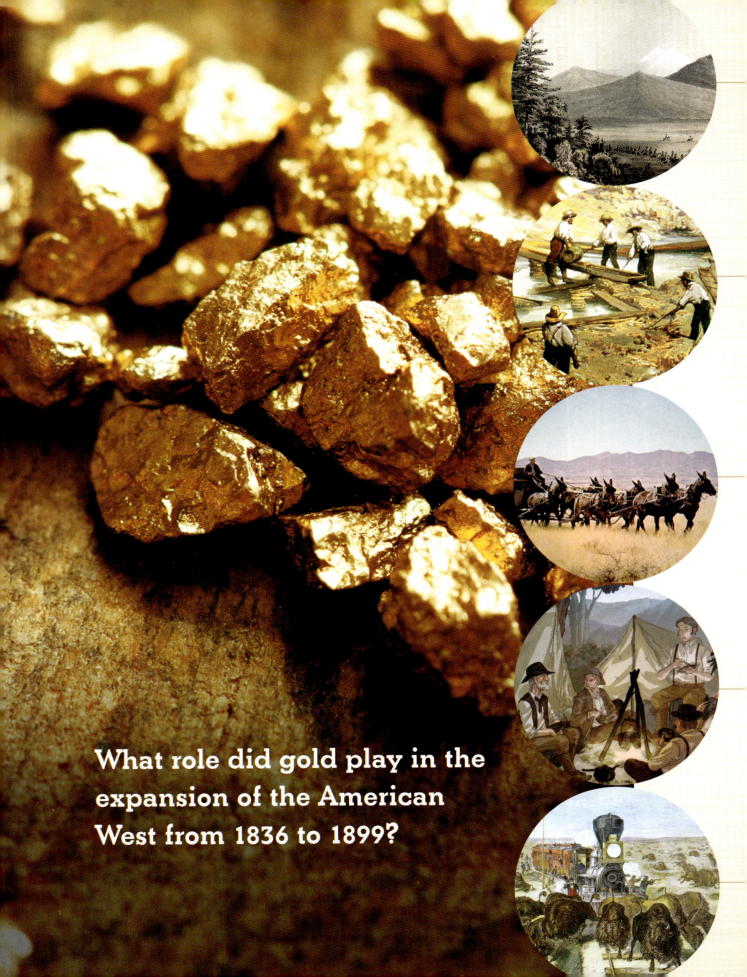

What role did gold play in the expansion of the American West from 1836 to 1899?

The Trail of Tears

In 1829, gold was discovered on Georgia land owned by the Cherokees. Many states in the South were eager to access the lands inhabited by Native Americans for many reasons, including laying claim to these riches, so Congress passed the Indian Removal Act of 1830.

Under the terms of this mandate, Native Americans were forced from their lands throughout the southeastern states. By 1839, U.S. soldiers had rounded up nearly 90,000 Choctaw, Cherokee, and others for a thousand-mile journey west. They traveled in boats, wagons, and on foot on what became known as the Trail of Tears. Thousands of Native Americans died along the way to their new lands in present-day Oklahoma, where their descendants live to this day.

≡ PERSONAL PERSPECTIVE ≡

"People feel bad when they leave old nation. Women cry and make sad wails. Children cry and many men cry, and all look sad like when friends die, but they say nothing and just put heads down and keep going toward the West."
—Survivor of the Trail of Tears

▲ The term Trail of Tears came from a Cherokee phrase *nunna-da-ul-tsun-yi*, which means "the trail where they cried."

≡ THE ROOT OF THE MEANING ≡

Mission generally means "a sending abroad." It stems from Latin *missionem*, or "act of sending, a release." In the 1500s, it was also referred to as a religious ministry commissioned to spread faith, or do humanitarian work.

▲ Along the Mormon Trail, the travelers pushed and pulled heavy handcarts.

The Texas Revolution

Beginning in the 1820s, U.S. settlers formed colonies in the part of northern Mexico known as Texas. In time, there were some 30,000 American Texans living there, and most were impatient with Mexico's government. They were mainly discontent because Mexico did not allow slavery and had tried to stop all American emigration to Texas. In 1835, the Texans revolted, demanding independence from Mexico.

In February 1836, approximately 180 Texans gathered in the Alamo, ready to defend San Antonio from 4,000 Mexican soldiers led by the proud General Antonio López de Santa Anna. As the Mexicans sacked the Alamo on March 6, 1836, all of the defenders were killed. On April 21, 1836, at San Jacinto, 900 Texans shouting "Remember the Alamo!" defeated 1,200 Mexicans. They soon captured General Santa Anna and the Republic of Texas was born.

Oregon Fever

American fascination with the West continued unabated. During the 1840s, Lieutenant John C. Frémont led a government expedition through the Rocky Mountains to California and Oregon Country. Soon a mass westward emigration began. People, like James Marshall, decided to leave their homes in the East and settle on the expanding Western frontier. They piled into trains, coaches, and steamboats to "jumping off" towns, such as Independence, Missouri. There, settlers bought wagons, mules, and oxen, and left the United States behind.

In May 1841, about 80 men, women, and children, including ex-trapper Tom Fitzpatrick and Catholic missionary Father Pierre-Jean De Smet, set out on the great trail to Oregon—the Oregon Trail. Some would turn south at Fort Hall, Idaho, and go to California. Either way, it took about six months to travel 3,200 kilometers (2,000 miles).

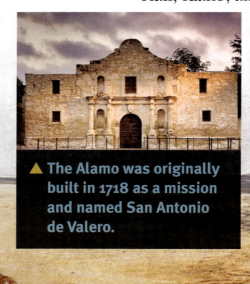

▲ The Alamo was originally built in 1718 as a mission and named San Antonio de Valero.

In 1842, only about 140 **emigrants** left the East and went west. But in the spring of 1843, 120 wagons, a huge herd of livestock, and as many as 1,000 pioneers headed out on the Oregon Trail. Between 1841 and 1869, 500,000 pioneers managed broken wagons, runaway teams of horses and oxen, flooded rivers, thunderstorms, stampeding bison, blizzards, and hunger along the Oregon Trail.

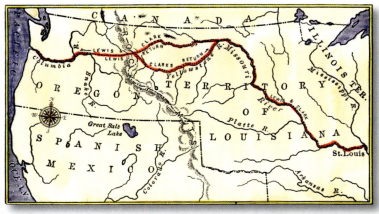

▲ Oregon Country, partly controlled by Great Britain, would eventually be divided into Oregon, Washington, Idaho, parts of Wyoming, and Montana in the United States, and British Columbia in Canada.

✔ CHECKPOINT
Read More About It
In your school library and/or online, read more about life on the overland trails, such as the Oregon Trail.

≡ PRIMARY SOURCES ≡
Catherine Sager Pringle

Among the hundreds who went west in 1844 was a girl around ten years old from Ohio named Catherine Sager, and her parents, two brothers, and four sisters. When she grew up, Catherine wrote about her adventure.

"Many friends came . . . and there was much sadness at the parting. . . . The motion of the wagon made us all sick, and it was weeks before we got used to the seasick motion. . . . Indians raided our camp one night and drove off a number of cattle. . . . Soon everything went smooth and our train made steady headway. . . . There were several musical instruments among the emigrants, and these sounded clearly on the evening air when camp was made. Merry talk and laughter resounded from almost every camp-fire."

Later on, Catherine's leg broke when her skirt caught in a wagon wheel. Even worse, her parents died along the trail. Once they reached the West, the seven Sager orphans were adopted by the missionaries, Marcus and Narcissa Whitman.

Manifest Destiny

Among those Americans who traveled west and those who stayed put, many truly believed that America's westward expansion was an important patriotic duty, a God-given destiny.

In 1844, the country elected James K. Polk to be the eleventh U.S. president. He pushed for the annexation of Texas and California, so they could become part of the Union. Within a year of his election, Texas became the 28th state. This addition strengthened the growing feeling that the U.S. should stretch across North America, from the Atlantic to the Pacific Ocean.

To achieve this goal, the United States would have to confront Great Britain, who shared the northern border out west between the U.S. and Canada.

It would also risk war, if Mexico refused to give up its southwestern territories, including California. In spite of the risks, many Americans thought it was their nation's **Manifest Destiny** to extend from sea to shining sea.

≡ HISTORICAL PERSPECTIVE ≡

Manifest Destiny

The writer who came up with the term "manifest destiny" was John L. O'Sullivan. In 1845, Mr. O'Sullivan wrote in the *Democratic Review*: "Our manifest destiny is to overspread the continent *allotted* by *Providence* (God) for the free development of our yearly multiplying millions [of people]."

▼ In his 1861 painting *Westward the Course of Empire Takes Its Way*, Emanuel Leutze illustrated his idea of westward expansion.

By 1846, President Polk had the political and popular support to unify the settlements in California and turn them against Mexico. Military explorer, John C. Frémont commanded U.S. troops in California. He built a fort in Monterey and raised a United States banner on the flagpole. Then, in June, some Californians did as the Texans had done ten years earlier: they declared their independence from Mexico and set up a republic. Soon their revolutionary "Bear Flag" fluttered over Sonoma, California. They were poised for a fight with the Mexican authorities, without even knowing that the U.S. Congress had already declared war on Mexico as of May 13, 1846. President Polk, determined to win California for the United States, had already sent troops that were ready to fight on the Santa Fe Trail. The Mexican-American War had begun.

≡THEY MADE A DIFFERENCE≡
President James Knox Polk
(1795–1849)

Small, stern James K. Polk and his nine younger siblings grew up in Tennessee. He became its governor in 1839, and a hard-working president in 1845. In winning the Mexican-American War, a large amount of territory was added to the United States, including California and most of the present-day Southwest—an area known

as the Mexican Cession. He also added the Oregon Territory after an agreement with the British, which altered the boundaries of the region.

▲ James K. Polk was the first president to be photographed in the White House. Photography was invented in 1839.

William L. Todd, nephew of future First Lady Mary Todd Lincoln, designed and made the first "Bear Flag," with a California grizzly bear and a lone star. The lone star was inspired by the Texans' flag. ▶

Republic of California

The Mexican Cession

In a battle near Los Angeles in January 1847, United States soldiers and sailors defeated the last armed Mexican resistance in California. On September 14, 1847, U.S. soldiers marched into Mexico City.

According to the peace **treaty** signed at Guadalupe Hidalgo on February 2, 1848, a defeated Mexico agreed to **cede**, or relinquish control of, 1,360,000 square kilometers (525,000 square miles) of land to the United States for $15 million. The area, known as the Mexican Cession, included California, Nevada, Utah, most of Arizona and New Mexico, and parts of Colorado and Wyoming.

◄ **Approximately 79,000 U.S. soldiers and sailors fought in the Mexican-American War.**

SUMMING UP

- Americans headed west to begin a new life, worship freely, convert Native Americans, and explore new frontiers.

- Not all those who traveled westward did so of their own free will. A government plan removed thousands of Native Americans from their lands, forcing them to relocate in the West. Thousands died along the Trail of Tears.

- The notion of Manifest Destiny excited the nation and provided support for Congress to declare war on Mexico. Victory in that war meant that the United States greatly increased its size and secured most of the land in the Southwest and California.

Putting It All Together

Choose one of the following research activities. Work independently, in pairs, or in small groups. Share your responses with your class, and listen to others present their work.

1 With a partner, imagine that you are living in the United States in the 1840s and you have come down with "Oregon Fever." Discuss and prepare a letter for your friends and family, telling them why you want to go to Oregon. Include ten items you will bring on your journey. Explain your choices.

2 Examine a map of the United States. Locate the juncture of the Missouri and Mississippi Rivers. Follow the Missouri River westward toward the Pacific Ocean. Describe the geographic features you would see on this journey. Specifically, write two first person point of view journal entries contrasting your trip across the Great Plains versus your trip across the Rocky Mountains.

3 On a current map of the United States, indicate areas that once belonged to Mexico. Specifically, indicate those lands acquired after Texan independence and the Mexican-American War (1846–1848). Describe the Mexican influence seen in these lands today (hint: names of people/towns, food, etc.).

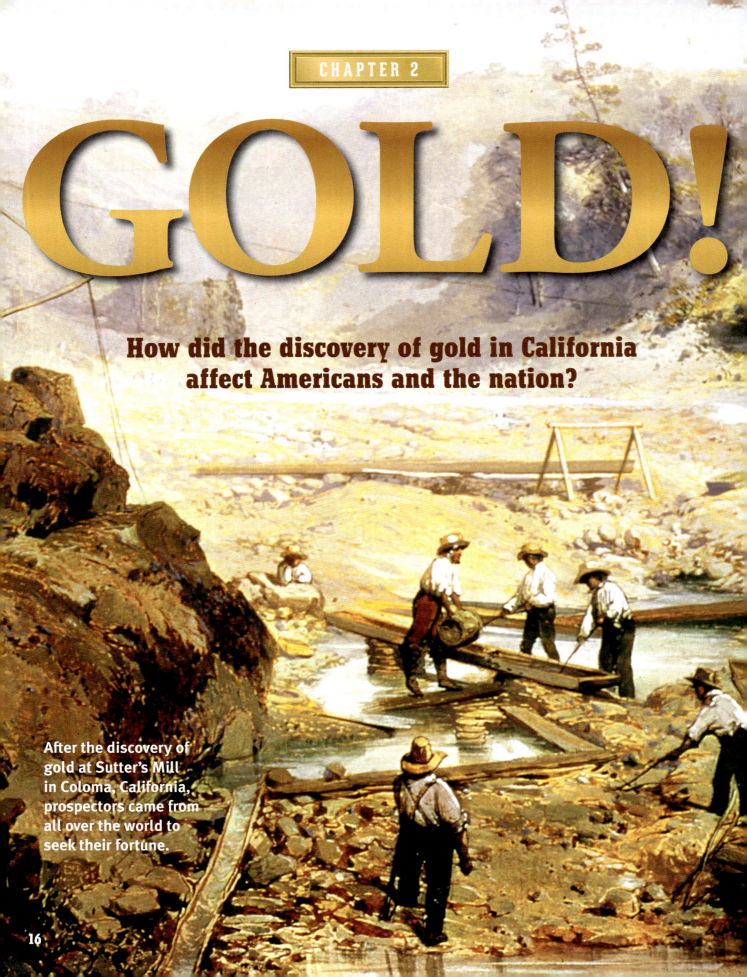

GOLD!

How did the discovery of gold in California affect Americans and the nation?

After the discovery of gold at Sutter's Mill in Coloma, California, prospectors came from all over the world to seek their fortune.

After James Marshall spotted gold in the American River, pioneers and prospectors came from across the nation. The reason is because gold is a scarce **commodity**, and therefore extremely valuable. In 1849, the U.S. dollar was backed by gold. At that time, one ounce of gold was worth about $16. (Today its value is nearly 100 times that amount). Those **prospectors** who did find gold often became very wealthy. Others came for gold, but instead made their fortunes making and selling goods to the miners. Levi Strauss sold them durable work pants, the first step toward his revolutionary product: blue jeans. Alexander H. Todd started a postal service. Instead of buying stamps, miners paid for mail delivery with gold dust.

Ironically, John Sutter and James Marshall did not fare as well. Sutter's farm workers and craftsmen all left to find gold. His fort's high walls could not keep gold-rushers from setting up tents on his land, trampling his crops, and butchering his cattle and sheep. He went bankrupt in 1852, never recovering his fortune. He died in 1880.

As a partner in Sutter's sawmill, James Marshall expected to be wealthy, but after his discovery, no one would work the mill. Moreover, he could not prove the legality of his mining claims. He lived out his life farming in California. He died in 1885.

By July 1848, Oregon settlers were flooding California. In August, it was estimated that nearly 4,000 miners were finding as much as $50,000 worth of gold *daily*. Then, on December 5, 1848, President Polk mentioned California's "abundance of gold" in his Fourth State of the Union Address, sparking a stampede of "**Forty-Niners**" in the early months of 1849. There would be other "rushes" for gold and silver, but none like the Gold Rush of 1849.

≡ HISTORY & ECONOMICS ≡
Commodity-Backed Currency

A commodity is a product of agriculture or mining that is valued and therefore bought and sold. Throughout history, many governments have used reserves of commodities to support the value of their currency, or legal tender.

For example, gold is a precious metal that is mined, and therefore a commodity. The gold standard is a monetary system in which the currency is based on a fixed quantity of gold held in reserve.

In the past, the United States has used silver, gold, and even tobacco to back the dollar. Today, no nation uses the gold standard. Instead the value of most currency is derived from the relationship between supply and demand rather than the value of the material that the money is made of.

Lansford Hastings' Emigrants' Guide to Oregon and California

Lansford Hastings advises pioneers on what they will need to pack:

"The emigrant should provide himself with, at least, 91 kilograms (200 pounds) of flour, or meal; 68 kilograms (150 pounds) of bacon; 5 kilograms (10 pounds) of coffee; 9 kilograms (20 pounds) of sugar; and 5 kilograms (10 pounds) of salt. . . . Very few cooking utensils should be taken, as they very much increase the load. . . . Blankets, sheets, coverlets and pillows, which, being spread upon a buffalo robe . . . or some other impervious (waterproof) substance, should constitute the beds."

The Forty-Niners

People spread far-fetched stories of California river bottoms being paved with gold, and nuggets laying about, waiting to be picked up. Eager shopkeepers sold tents, equipment, and hastily written guidebooks to crowds of would-be millionaires. Getting to the gold fields, however, was a huge challenge. Many sailed down the Atlantic Ocean, crossed 48 kilometers (30 miles) of Panama jungle, then waited for a ship to take them up the Pacific Ocean, to San Francisco.

Forty-Niners poured into Eastern and Southern seaports and scrambled aboard any sort of vessel that would get them to California. ▶

How to Pan for Gold

Panning for gold meant sifting and separating bits of gold from sandy, gravelly dirt. The miners came up with many clever devices to speed up the process, but the simplest, most popular piece of equipment was a shallow pan.

Fill your pan with dirt. Swirl it about in a stream. The water washes out all but the relatively heavy gold. You have hit "pay dirt!" In 1849 in San Francisco, an ounce of gold flakes, dust, or nuggets, was worth $16. You can look up the current value of gold to calculate what an ounce would be worth today.

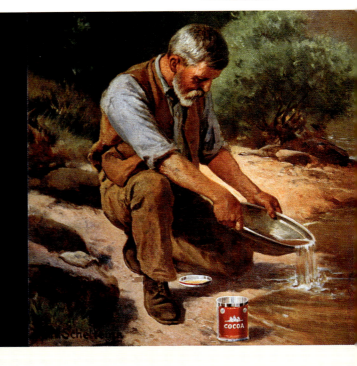

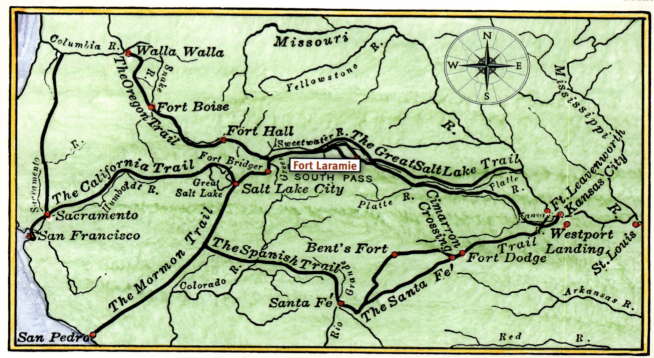

▲ Taking the trails from Fort Laramie could take up to nine months.

Other Eastern Americans arrived there, having sailed down around the southern tip of South America, braving violent ocean storms, then all the way north to the seaport. With luck and good weather, the 20,930-kilometer (13,000-mile) voyage took about nine months.

Thousands of gold-rushers took southern routes to California, either by the Santa Fe Trail, through Arizona, or by the Old Spanish Trail, up into Utah and then down to Los Angeles. Then they hurried north to the Sacramento Valley.

Many of California's Native Americans were made to work the gold mines for little or no money. Thousands died from illnesses contracted from white gold seekers. Their environment suffered, too. By 1852, surface gold had been taken, so miners instead dug into, tore up, and shot water at the land, causing terrible erosion and pollution.

≡ HISTORICAL PERSPECTIVE ≡
Gold Rush!

On May 29, 1848, San Franciscans saw this in their copy of *The Californian*:

"The whole country from San Francisco to Los Angeles, and from the sea shore to the base of the Sierra Nevada, resounds with the sordid cry of 'Gold, gold, gold!' while the field is left half-planted, the house half built, and everything neglected but the manufacture of shovels and pickaxes."

The gold-rushers' germs killed many Plains Indians as well. Gold-rusher wagons and hungry animals left the prairie rutted, with no grass for the bison, on which the Native Americans depended.

New Faces of the West

Of the thousands who traveled to California to seek gold, many were Chinese immigrants. They called California *Gum Shan*, which translates as "Gold Mountain." After giving up on gold prospecting, many Chinese people settled in San Francisco, working as merchants, cooks, and laundry workers. Despite cruel treatment from whites, the Chinese community flourished there. Many other Chinese would later work on the railroad.

Many African Americans also became Forty-Niners. The first black miners were free sailors. Most abandoned their whaling ships in San Francisco and made their way to the gold fields of California. Within two years there were over 1,000 and at the end of four years there were more than 2,000. Of the hundreds of enslaved African Americans who also came to California, some found enough gold to buy their freedom.

▲ Civil war, famines, and poverty made for a hard life in China. California seemed full of golden promise.

✔

≡ CHECKPOINT ≡

Make Connections

Why do people emigrate? Where are your ancestors from and why may they have moved or relocated in the past?

▲ To keep the Union together, Kentucky Senator Henry Clay proposed the Compromise of 1850.

The Compromise of 1850

There were major changes throughout the nation following the discovery of gold in California. In March 1849, former general Zachary Taylor became president. Within a year he was dead, and Vice President Millard Fillmore became president. Gold-seekers had enlarged California's population by many thousands, within just a year. By law, only 60,000 citizens were required before a territory could become a state. Although it was inevitable that California would become a state, questions remained about its status in regard to slavery.

The question sparked months of arguments between powerful, angry senators from the pro-slavery South and others from the anti-slavery North. The political battle threatened to pull the nation apart and lead to war. To keep the peace, Congress produced a set of laws called the Compromise of 1850.

Among other things, the compromise made it easier to catch "fugitive" slaves—ones who had fled the South to freedom—and return them to their owners. Also, no longer could slaves be bought and sold in Washington, D.C. And as of September 9, 1850, California was admitted into the Union as a free state.

The argument over slavery would intensify in the following years. As with many compromises, few people were completely pleased. However, there were thousands of cheering Californians once they received the news of their statehood.

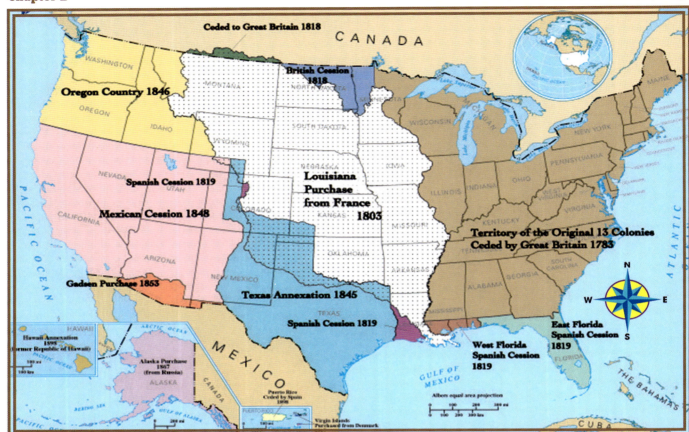

▲ The U.S. border with Mexico was finally settled with the Gadsden Purchase in 1853.

New Territories and New Troubles

In 1852, the peak year of the gold rush, nearly 70,000 people went west on the trails, and Americans elected Franklin Pierce as president. One of his concerns was the border between the United States and Mexico, still unsettled since the war. President Pierce asked diplomat James Gadsden to negotiate in Mexico. The talks led to the Gadsden Purchase of 1853. The United States paid Mexico $10 million for 76,770 square kilometers (29,640 square miles) of land, in what is now southern New Mexico and Arizona. Mexican President López de Santa Anna agreed to the purchase because he felt the United States was going to seize it anyway.

Kansas and Nebraska proved to be a thornier matter. In May 1854, the U.S. Congress organized much of the Great Plains into the Kansas and Nebraska Territories. As to whether or not slavery would be allowed there, Illinois Senator Stephen A. Douglas proposed that the local settlers vote on it in each territory. This was known as **popular sovereignty**. Encouraging pioneers to settle the western territories meant the promise of new states, and new voters. Controlling Congress, and the legality of slavery, would depend on those votes. Slaveholders were not likely to settle in the more northern Nebraska Territory, but the large Kansas Territory was right next to slave-holding Missouri.

Those Missourians who wanted slavery to spread west had only to cross the border and vote for it. Hundreds of American **abolitionists**, who sought to end slavery and free all enslaved laborers, hurried to Kansas from as far away as New England to vote against slavery.

Soon deadly violence broke out along the Missouri-Kansas border. It was a preview of what was to come—a war that would divide the nation. But by then, the 1849 California Gold Rush would be a memory, replaced by a rush for riches in the far-western Kansas Territory, which is present-day Colorado.

SUMMING UP

- The discovery of gold at Sutter's Mill in 1848 drew hundreds of thousands of prospectors to California. Few struck it rich panning for gold, but some capitalized on the needs of the miners.

- The faces of the American West began to change as Chinese emigrants and African Americans poured into California.

- The debate over free and slave states heated up as California became part of the Union and the Gadsden Purchase increased U.S.-owned lands.

Putting It All Together

Choose one of the following research activities. Work independently, in pairs, or in small groups. Share your responses with your class, and listen to others present their work.

1 Imagine that you are living in the United States in 1849 and want to make your way west to find gold. Draw a map of the United States and its surrounding territories at the time. Then plan and mark your route.

2 In the early California gold rush, mining supplies were scarce. A saying about this period was, "The miners mined the mine, but the merchants mined the miners." What do you think this means? Research and write a short essay explaining the relevance of this quote and use text evidence to support your interpretation.

3 Read more about the issue of slavery and the Compromise of 1850, and write a persuasive essay that explains why it was a successful or unsuccessful piece of government legislation. Cite text evidence to support your claims.

A CHANGING NATION

What events took place as gold was discovered throughout the West?

In 1860, a presidential election year, it grew more likely that the new president, as commander in chief, might have to wage war to preserve the Union. At this critical time, citizens' need for information sparked huge progress in the areas of transportation and communication. From stagecoaches to Pony Express riders, to telegraph wires, to the Transcontinental Railroad, Americans wanted and needed ways to stay connected from coast to coast.

The Stagecoach Era

There were many stagecoach lines. In the mid-1850s, they competed for the right (and government funds) to provide postal service between the Eastern and Western United States. In 1857, John Butterfield's company was chosen. Eventually, it purchased some 2,000 horses and mules and 250 **stagecoaches**. An army of workers was hired to build 139 relay stations and run the Butterfield Overland Mail. The "stages" would make regular, scheduled trips from Tipton, Missouri, down through Arkansas, Texas, across the southwestern desert, then up to San Francisco, California—some 4,505 kilometers (2,800 miles) in twenty-five days or less!

As the 1850s ended, westerners got their newspapers off the Butterfield Overland Mail stagecoaches. They read about the increasingly angry political news—and that gold *and* silver continued to be found all over the West.

▼ They were called stagecoaches because every ten to fifteen miles, the driver stopped for passengers and to exchange his tired horses for fresh ones, for the next stage of the journey.

≡ HISTORICAL PERSPECTIVE ≡

The Concord Coach

The wooden, 1,134-kilogram (2,500-pound) Concord Coach was suspended over the wheels and axles on leather strap braces. Nine passengers could ride in a large coach, with a dozen more up on the roof! The driver managed the three or four pairs of horses or mules that pulled a Concord Coach, at about 15 kilometers per hour (9 miles per hour). Some say that the term "riding shotgun" came from the shotgun-toting conductor, who sat up beside the driver, also armed, in case of bandits.

≡ PRIMARY SOURCES ≡

All Aboard the Butterfield Mail!

When the first Butterfield Overland Mail stagecoach pulled out of Tipton, Missouri, in September 1858, it carried newspaper reporter Waterman L. Ormsby, who paid the $200 fare to ride all the way to San Francisco. Ormsby's account of the ride was published in the Sunday *New York Herald* on October 14, 1858. Here he describes a road near Fayetteville, Arkansas:

"Our road was steep, rugged, jagged, rough, and mountainous—and then wish for some more expressive words in the language. . . . The wiry, light little [mules] tugged and pulled as if they would tear themselves to pieces, and our heavy wagon bounded along the crags as if it would be shaken to pieces, and ourselves disemboweled on the spot."

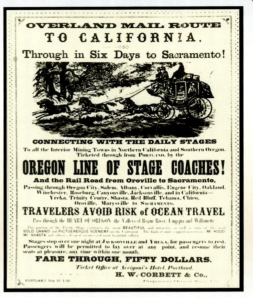

▲ Butterfield Overland Mail advertisement

The Wild West

Ten years after James Marshall's discovery, gold was found in the future states of Colorado, Idaho, Montana, and Nevada. A prospector named Jake Snively found success in the New Mexico Territory, sparking a gold rush to the Gila River (in present-day Arizona). Even as prospectors hurried off to the southwest desert, others raced to the Rocky Mountains region because William "Green" Russell found gold where Denver, Colorado, is now located. Easterners headed to Colorado painted "Pikes Peak or Bust!" on their wagons.

Yet another gold rush began in 1859, east of the Sierra Nevada Mountains (in present-day Nevada). Two fellows spied gold not far from where the Donner Party, a group of emigrants traveling west, were trapped by heavy snowfall only thirteen years earlier. Then a **lode** of silver was found in Utah. This naturally forming deposit of metal **ore** turned up a curious blueish mud as prospectors worked with their picks and shovels. The mud was full of silver ore. This tremendously rich find became known as the Comstock Lode.

Soon, muddy, messy mining camps were popping up. As miners crowded into the rowdy saloons in towns like Virginia City, Nevada, many more poured into the Clearwater Mountains, way up in the future state of Idaho. Elias D. Pierce discovered gold there in October 1860, just weeks before the U.S. presidential election. Towns grew overnight, too fast to organize local systems of government and law enforcement. The result was rampant crime and lawlessness, which is how the "Wild West" got its name.

▲ A Pony Express rider carried the mail in the pockets of a leather *mochila*.

The Pony Express

On April 3, 1860, after a whirlwind of preparations, three Missouri businessmen, William H. Russell, Alexander Majors, and William B. Waddell, launched the famous Pony Express. Crowds in San Francisco, California, and St. Joseph, Missouri, 3,165 kilometers (1,966 miles) away, cheered as the first two riders sped off. At relay stations, 16 to 24 kilometers (10 to 15 miles) apart, riders jumped off their tired steeds, grabbed their *mochilas*, (a Spanish word for knapsacks) tossed them over the saddles of fresh horses and galloped away. Eastbound and westbound riders passed one another on the historic trip—accomplished in 10 days! But electric messages outraced the ponies. In October 1861, when telegraph wires stretched across the continent, the Pony Express was no longer in business.

▼ The Pony Express ran this ad: "Wanted: Young, skinny, wiry, fellows. Not over eighteen. Must be expert riders willing to risk death daily. Orphans preferred. Wages $25 per week."

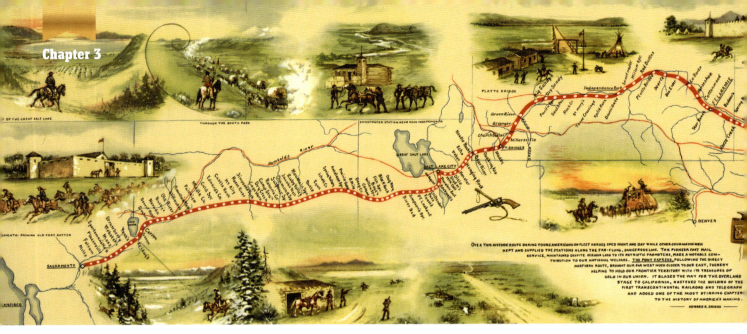

▲ Before the Pony Express, news could take months to travel across the country. The Pony Express allowed messages to travel as quickly as ten days. However, it was no match for the telegraph, which could send electric messages in minutes. After only one year, the Pony Express was rendered obsolete.

≡HISTORY & LITERATURE≡

Roughing It

In his 1872 book *Roughing It*, Samuel Clemens, aka Mark Twain, described the rider he saw on his trip west in the 1860s:

"The pony-rider was usually a little bit of a man, brimful of spirit and endurance. No matter what time of the day or night his watch came on, and no matter whether it was winter or summer, raining, snowing, hailing, or sleeting, or whether his 'beat' was a level straight road or a crazy trail over mountain crags . . . or whether it led through peaceful regions or regions that swarmed with hostile Indians, he must be always ready to leap into the saddle and be off like the wind!"

The Civil War

Shortly after President Abraham Lincoln was elected in 1860, eleven southern states **seceded** from the Union and formed the Confederate States of America. The Civil War began on April 12, 1861, when Confederate soldiers fired on U.S. Fort Sumter, in Charleston, South Carolina. Prospecting continued despite and throughout the bloody, tragic Civil War.

In 1862, gold began to be mined in the future state of Montana, while thousands of Union and Confederate soldiers died on battlefields from Tennessee to Maryland. In 1863, President Lincoln issued the Emancipation Proclamation, freeing all enslaved peoples in states and other areas not under Union control. In doing so, he made the Civil War a fight for human freedom as well as for restoring the Union. The war ended in 1865, when Confederate General Robert E. Lee surrendered to Union General Ulysses S. Grant.

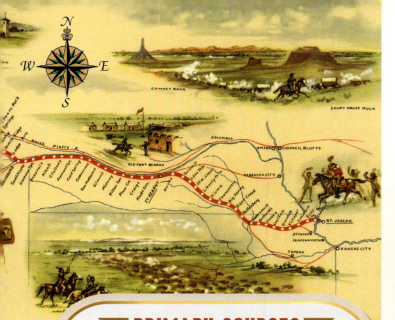

Indian Wars

Many soldiers of the Civil War joined U.S. militia already fighting native tribes of the West. As they had since colonial days, Indians often fought back when newcomers threatened their traditional ways of life and treated them unfairly. The Cheyenne and Arapahos of the southern plains fought to protect themselves until government officials forced them onto a reservation along Sand Creek, in barren, eastern Colorado. A Cheyenne chief, Black Kettle, tried to make peace, but in the cold dawn of November 29, 1864, Colonel John M. Chivington and about 650 men attacked Black Kettle's settlement and killed 133 people, mostly women and children.

> "We are different nations, but it seems as if we were but one people, whites and all."
>
> — Black Kettle (1803–1868)

There were other troubles along the Bozeman Trail, which snaked through the wilds north of Fort Laramie up to the Montana mining towns—and directly through Lakota Sioux hunting lands. Ever more wagons disturbed the bison as well as the Oglala-Lakota Sioux. Work was well underway on a massive project that would change their world more than any trail or rush for gold: the Transcontinental Railroad.

≡ PRIMARY SOURCES ≡

Black Kettle's Letter

Black Kettle's people lived in western Kansas and eastern Colorado. Three months before the Sand Creek Massacre, in a letter to the local government, he wrote:

"Sir: We held a council . . . and all came to the conclusion to make peace with you providing you make peace with the Kiowas, Comanches, Arapahos, Apaches, and Sioux. We are going to send a message to the Kiowas . . . about our going to make [peace] with you. . . . We heard that you [have] some prisoners in Denver. We have seven prisoners of yours, which we are willing to give up, providing you give up yours . . . we want true news from you in return."

Black Kettle survived the Sand Creek Massacre, but he was later killed in an attack by General George A. Custer's 7th U.S. Cavalry, on November 27, 1868.

The Long Railroad

In 1862, President Lincoln signed legislation, authorizing land and loans for work to be done on the Transcontinental Railroad. The Union Pacific Railroad would build tracks west, out of Omaha, Nebraska. Eastward from Sacramento, California, the Central Pacific Railroad would build tracks over and through the impossibly rugged mountains. Eventually, the two tracks would meet, but it would take armies of laborers to accomplish this huge undertaking! They had no steam shovels, jackhammers, or bulldozers. They had only human and animal muscle, picks, shovels—and "Patent Blasting Oil," made with nitroglycerin. They used it to blast out mountain tunnels.

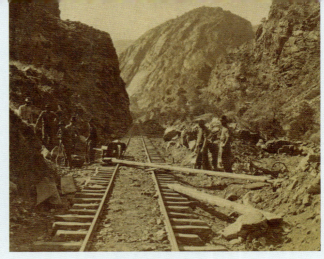

▲ To complete the Transcontinental Railroad, workers had to blast through the Sierra Nevada Mountains.

So many men were off prospecting for gold that the Central Pacific hired Chinese immigrants, despite people's racist attitudes at the time. Many of the Chinese had come originally looking for gold. Others now came for the opportunity to work for the railroad. They did much of the backbreaking, dangerous work on the western railroad.

The tracks met at last, on May 10, 1869, at Promontory, Utah. Countless iron spikes had been hammered down to hold the railroad ties on 2,858 kilometers (1,776 miles) of track.

✔ CHECKPOINT
Visualize

Imagine crossing the country in different ways. How did railroad travel differ from travel by horse and wagon?

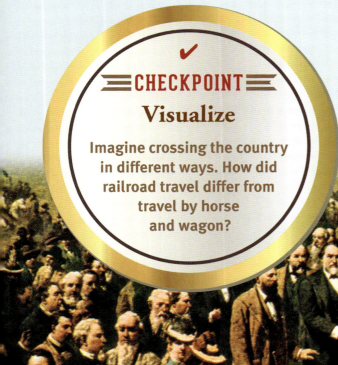

▲ At the ceremony connecting the two railroad lines, men pounded down a special spike—the very last. It was made of gold.

SUMMING UP

- Gold and large deposits of silver ore continued to be discovered throughout the west and southwest.

- As the slavery question pushed the nation toward the Civil War, Americans on both sides of the country saw the need to be connected. New ventures that brought opposite shores of the United States together included the stagecoach, Pony Express, telegraph, and the Transcontinental Railroad. Chinese immigrants were instrumental in building the western half of that railroad.

- The Union was preserved as the South surrendered in 1865, but bloodshed continued as the U.S. Army decimated Native American tribes throughout the Great Plains.

Putting It All Together

Choose one of the following research activities. Work independently, in pairs, or in small groups. Share your responses with your class, and listen to others present their work.

1 Read the list of names of actual gold mining towns in California around 1850: Get Up and Git; Grizzly Flats; Old Dry Diggings; Hangtown; Rough and Ready; and Poverty Hill. Based on your knowledge of the gold rush, select (or pick from a hat) one of the towns from the list, and write a story explaining how you think the town got its name. Be creative, yet historically accurate.

2 Research communication and technology in the 1860s. Make a map of the United States during this period that indicates: a) the route of the Butterfield Overland Mail stagecoach from Tipton, Missouri, to San Francisco, California, in 1858; b) the route of the Pony Express in 1861 (from St. Louis, Missouri, to San Francisco); c) the first Western Union telegraph line in 1862; and d) the route of the Transcontinental Railroad in 1869 (from Omaha, Nebraska, to San Francisco). Indicate the impact of each innovation in the West.

3 Reread pages 27–28. List five qualifications required to be a Pony Express rider. Explain why the Pony Express wanted these qualifications for its riders. Then write a short diary entry from the perspective of a young rider.

GOLD RUSH JUSTICE

CARTOONIST'S NOTEBOOK BY DENIS O'ROURKE AND HEIDI WARD. ILLUSTRATED BY ALEX CANAS

DURING THE GOLD RUSH, MANY PEOPLE TRAVELED ACROSS THE COUNTRY TO SEARCH FOR GOLD IN THE WEST.

NEIL CAME WEST TO SEEK HIS FORTUNE DURING THE GOLD RUSH. HE LEARNED QUICKLY HOW DIFFERENT LIFE HERE WAS COMPARED TO BACK EAST.

THERE WERE NO POLICE OR COURTS OR EVEN JAILS. ORDER WAS MAINTAINED BY A GROUP OF VIGILANTES.

THE MINERS GREW TO TRUST HIM.

WE'D LIKE YOU TO LEAD THE VIGILANTE COMMITTEE, NEIL.

SHOULD NEIL LET THE MAN GO WITH A WARNING?

OR SHOULD HE PUNISH HIM AS A WAY TO KEEP ORDER IN THIS DANGEROUS TOWN?

EXPLAIN YOUR ANSWER.

CHAPTER 4

THE GREAT COST OF GOLD

Railroad workers were paid to shoot bison that interfered with railway passage.

How did the rush for riches change the United States and the lives of Native Americans?

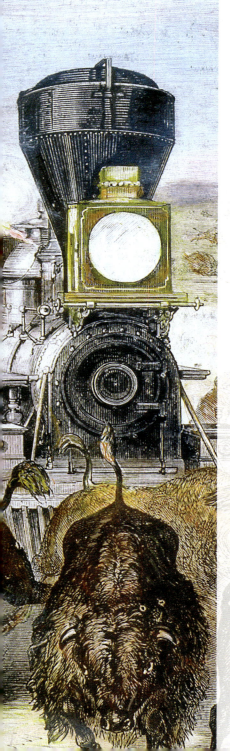

The Transcontinental Railroad brought an end to the Plains Indians' way of life as the great herds of bison that supplied their food and shelter were killed by ever-increasing numbers of newcomers to the West. Meanwhile, the Cheyenne, Arapaho, and other native peoples were pushed into smaller and smaller territories. Their culture clashed with that of white settlers, who wanted to mine, farm, and set up ranches on the land. By the 1870s, there were rumors of gold in the Black Hills of present-day South Dakota. Despite the government's promises to stay off their lands, an expedition was ordered into the sacred home country of the Sioux.

The Black Hills Gold Rush

In July 1874, General George A. Custer led a long wagon train out of Fort Abraham Lincoln near present-day Mandan, North Dakota. The expedition soon discovered gold in French Creek in the Black Hills. Custer sent a fast rider east with the news, which was then telegraphed to the world. Despite half-hearted attempts to stop them, prospectors rushed to the Black Hills.

In 1875, President Ulysses S. Grant offered Sioux Chief Red Cloud and other leaders a large sum of money for the Black Hills. They refused. They also turned down an annual payment of $400,000 to let thousands of gold-seekers **prospect** safely on their land. The miners came anyway, and attacks on both Native Americans and settlers continued. The U.S. government eventually sent an army to relocate the Sioux and other tribes by force. Native American leaders such as Crazy Horse and Sitting Bull prepared for war. It soon raged from the Black Hills to the northern prairies.

Native American Resistance

The Battle of Little Bighorn

General Custer's 7th U.S. Cavalry arrived at the Little Bighorn River in Southeastern Montana where thousands of Sioux and other native groups were gathered against the government's orders. They were tired of conforming to the government's policies and broken treaties. Custer's troops rode into battle, surprised that they were so outnumbered by native forces. Sitting Bull, a holy man of the Lakota Sioux tribe, had earlier envisioned the soldiers' defeat, and so it was: Custer and the 265 men under his command were killed that day, June 25, 1876.

▲ Low Dog

≡ PRIMARY SOURCES ≡

Eyewitness Account

In July 1881, Oglala Sioux Chief Low Dog gave his account of the Battle of Little Bighorn:

"They came on us like a thunderbolt. I never . . . saw men so brave and fearless as those white warriors. . . I called to my men, 'This is a good day to die: follow me.' . . . As we rushed upon them, the white warriors dismounted to fire, but they did very poor shooting. They held their horses' reins on one arm while they were shooting, but their horses were so frightened that they pulled the men all around. . . . Everything was in confusion. . . . I did not see General Custer. I do not know who killed him. We did not know till the fight was over that he was the white chief."

▼ George Armstrong Custer was a flashy, ambitious veteran of the Civil War.

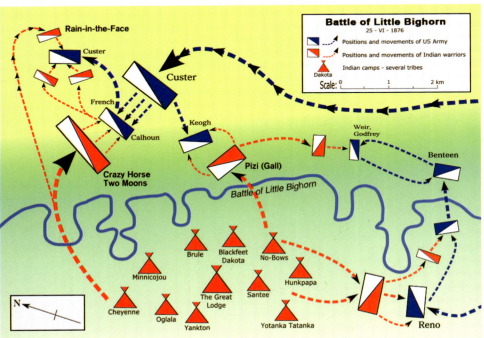

▲ Custer was killed at the Battle of Little Bighorn in 1876.

▼ Sitting Bull
(1831–1890)

"When I was a boy the Sioux owned the world; the sun rose and set on their land." — Sitting Bull

Sitting Bull

In 1876, Americans marking the nation's 100th birthday reacted to news of "Custer's Last Stand" at the Battle of Little Bighorn with fury. Thousands of soldiers were sent west to subdue the Native Americans once and for all. Though native warriors won many battles, soldiers kept the Native Americans from hunting dwindling numbers of bison. In the spring of 1877, the starving Sioux were forced to surrender. As government forces took over the Black Hills, Sitting Bull led a band of his people to Canada. The Sioux warrior, Crazy Horse, turned himself in. He was killed by a soldier in September 1877.

In 1881, Sitting Bull surrendered himself and his starving people to U.S. authorities. After two years of imprisonment, Sitting Bull was released.

≡ HISTORICAL PERSPECTIVE ≡

Sitting Bull

In 1884, just released from prison, Sitting Bull was allowed to spend some weeks touring eastern cities with the fabulously popular Buffalo Bill's Wild West Show, run by former Pony Express rider, gold-rusher, and bison hunter, "Buffalo Bill" Cody. Sitting Bull shook hands with President Grover Cleveland and made friends with the show's star attraction, sharpshooter Annie Oakley. Sitting Bull called her *Watanya Cecilia*—Little Sure Shot.

MISS ANNIE OAKLEY
(LITTLE SURE SHOT)
CABINET PORTRAIT

≡ CHECKPOINT ≡

Talk About It

In the Black Hills of South Dakota are four U.S. presidents carved onto Mount Rushmore. Fewer than 20 miles away is a sculpture of Crazy Horse. Why are both of these monuments important?

The Nez Perce War

Far to the west, the Nez Perce Indians (or Nimi'ipuu, as they call themselves) faced their own crisis. In 1855, the Nez Perce had signed the Wallowa treaty with the U.S. government, giving up their land and agreeing to move to a **reservation** in the Oregon Territory. But when gold was discovered three years later on the Oregon reservation, whites arrived almost immediately to prospect and settle. Instead of the federal government honoring the terms of the treaty, in May 1877, bands of Nez Perce were ordered out of Oregon's Wallowa Valley.

Chief Joseph and others knew they must go if they were to have peace, so they rounded up their livestock and began a trek to find freedom in Canada. From June to October, violence broke out and there were many casualties. Eventually, the Nez Perce were prevented from getting to Canada and were split up. Chief Joseph surrendered to U.S. forces on October 5, 1877, just 40 miles from the Canada border. Of the nearly 750 Nez Perce who began their 2,254-kilometer (1,400-mile) trek, only 334 women and children and 79 men were still alive. Chief Joseph was imprisoned, then sent to a reservation in Washington, where he died in 1904.

≡ HISTORICAL PERSPECTIVE ≡

Chief Joseph

Chief Joseph had been educated as a boy by the missionaries Henry and Eliza Spalding, who came west with the Whitmans in 1836. The following speech that Chief Joseph gave upon his surrender on October 5, 1877 was widely distributed.

"I am tired of fighting. . . . The old men are all dead. . . . The little children are freezing. . . . My people, some of them, have run away to the hills, and have no blankets, no food. No one knows where they are—perhaps freezing to death. I want to have time to look for my children. . . . Maybe I shall find them among the dead. . . . I am tired. My heart is sick and sad. From where the sun now stands I will fight no more forever."

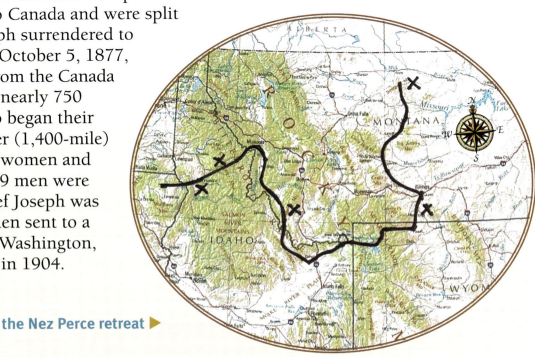

the Nez Perce retreat ▶

The Last of the Apaches

After their leader Cochise died in 1874, the government changed its treaty with the Chiricahua Apaches of southern Arizona. Now, instead of in their mountains, the tribe had to crowd onto a barren reservation, where they were expected to learn English and follow white customs. One warrior escaped into Mexico. His name was Geronimo (*Goyathlay*).

From his mountain hideout, Geronimo launched attacks on white settlers and soldiers in both Mexico and the U.S. He earned a reputation as a fearsome renegade who fought to keep the free life he was born to. Faced with a 5,000-man army, Geronimo surrendered in 1886. He spent years in various jails before he was sent to Fort Sill in Oklahoma, where he died in 1909. At that time, almost all Native Americans were living on reservations.

▲ Geronimo

Wounded Knee Massacre

During the 1880s, as the U.S. government continued to seize more and more hunting lands, some tribes took comfort and courage from a religion that promised the return of their old ways, lost loved ones, and the bison. Believers performed a prayer ceremony known as the "Ghost Dance."

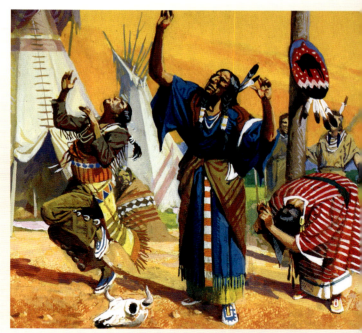

▲ **For the Ghost Dance, dancers shuffled their feet slowly, then ever faster, around and around.**

In 1890, the Ghost Dance movement began to take hold on reservations. Authorities saw the related gatherings as a threat, fearing the dances would incite violence. As more Native Americans spoke out about why they were performing the ritual, authorities took precautions. The Bureau of Indian Affairs called for extra soldiers and the arrest of influential holy man Sitting Bull, of the Lakota Sioux tribe.

On December 15, 1890, Sitting Bull was killed in the fight between the arresting officers and his protectors. With tensions high, the government sent the 7th Cavalry to surround the remaining Lakota camped at Wounded Knee Creek in southwestern South Dakota. On December 29, 1890, the cavalry massacred hundreds of Indian men, women, and children.

Rushes to the North

In the summer of 1896, when three men spied gold near the Klondike River in Canada's Yukon Territory, prospectors nearby got very rich. In July 1897, about 3,220 kilometers (2,000 miles) away, ships loaded with Klondike gold steamed into San Francisco and Seattle; then another gold rush began.

Gold-seekers poured into Skagway, Alaska, still a great distance from the Klondike River. Of the hundred thousand men who traveled to Alaska, only about 30,000 made it to the Klondike River and most experienced great hardship. Many turned back, were robbed by outlaws, froze or starved to death, along with their overloaded pack animals. Some eventually reached Bennett Lake, where they could then go 500 miles down the Yukon River to the gold fields. On this last phase of the trip, hundreds died navigating the rapids downstream. Few out-of-towners got rich in the Klondike Gold Rush. The gold was deep below the surface, under snow and ice, and most claims had been staked by the time many gold-seekers arrived.

In 1899, the nineteenth century saw one more gold rush on the far western coast of Alaska in Nome. The population of this small town along the Snake River increased to about 10,000 that first year. Gold was easy to find, laying along the beaches and shallow waters of the coastline. By 1909, the gold rush was over. The population of 20,000 dwindled, as it did in many

boom towns. Today the current population in Nome is less than 4,000.

At a terrible cost, and with tremendous effort, the nation had expanded westward, to the Pacific Ocean and beyond. There were many reasons for the United States to settle the West, but nothing propelled this expansion faster than people's hunger for gold.

≡ HISTORY & LITERATURE ≡
The Call of the Wild

Jack London's adventures in the Klondike Gold Rush inspired his popular adventure story *The Call of the Wild* (1903), about a sled-dog named Buck. Here is how it begins:

"Buck did not read the newspapers, or he would have known that trouble was brewing, not alone for himself, but for every tidewater dog, strong of muscle and with warm, long hair, from Puget Sound to San Diego. Because men, groping in the Arctic darkness, had found a yellow metal, . . . thousands of men were rushing into the Northland. These men wanted dogs, and the dogs they wanted were heavy dogs, with strong muscles by which to toil, and furry coats to protect them from the frost."

SUMMING UP

- The Transcontinental Railroad contributed to the end of the Native Americans' food source, bison, and their way of life. The government moved more Indians onto reservations.

- Gold was discovered in the Black Hills of South Dakota in the 1870s, bringing government treaties and military action against the Sioux tribes.

- The last great gold rushes of the century brought miners to the Yukon Territory in Canada and Nome, Alaska.

Putting It All Together

Choose one of the following research activities. Work independently, in pairs, or in small groups. Share your responses with your class, and listen to others present their work.

1 Using resources in your school library, prepare a report in which you show (with drawings) and tell how the Plains Indians lived, what they ate, how they dressed, how they traveled, etc.

2 The Transcontinental Railroad transformed the American West. Instead of sailing around the dangerous seas of Cape Horn for a four- to six-month journey to San Francisco, easterners could now travel safely to California in only six days. Describe the social, economic, and political impact it had on the West.

3 In the famous play "Inherit the Wind," the main character states, "Gentlemen, progress has never been a bargain, you have to pay for it." So it was with the gold rush and the settling of the West. Explain, in a short essay, some examples of progress from this time period. Then explain an example of how certain people paid for this progress.

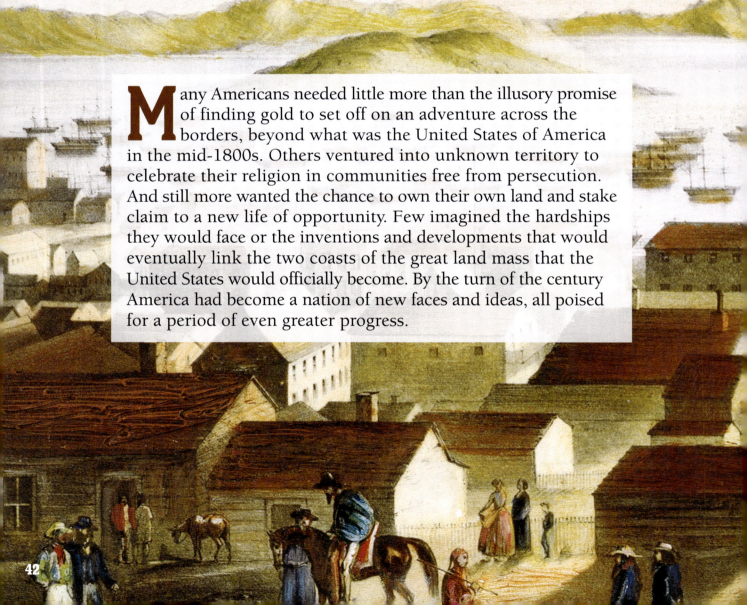

GOLD
THE GREAT CATALYST

Many Americans needed little more than the illusory promise of finding gold to set off on an adventure across the borders, beyond what was the United States of America in the mid-1800s. Others ventured into unknown territory to celebrate their religion in communities free from persecution. And still more wanted the chance to own their own land and stake claim to a new life of opportunity. Few imagined the hardships they would face or the inventions and developments that would eventually link the two coasts of the great land mass that the United States would officially become. By the turn of the century America had become a nation of new faces and ideas, all poised for a period of even greater progress.

Time Line

●	**1841**	Trappers guide the first wagon train to Oregon.
●	**1842–1846**	John C. Frémont explores the West.
●	**1843**	the migration on the Oregon Trail
●	**1845**	The United States annexes Texas.
●	**1846**	Britain cedes southern part of Oregon Territory to the U.S.
●	**1846–1848**	Mexican-American War
●	**1847**	Initial group of Mormons migrate to Utah.
●	**1848**	U.S. wins western lands from Mexico. California gold is discovered.
●	**1849**	Thousands of Forty-Niners rush to California.
●	**1850**	California becomes a state.
●	**1853**	the Gadsden Purchase
●	**1854**	Easterners rush into Kansas Territory.
●	**1859**	A series of gold rushes begin throughout the West; silver is discovered in abundance at the Comstock Lode mine.
●	**1860–1861**	Pony Express riders carry U.S. mail from western Missouri to the far West.
●	**1861**	Telegraph wires connect California with the East.
●	**1861–1865**	The Civil War rages.
●	**1862**	Gold is discovered in Montana; the Sioux Uprising occurs.
●	**1863–1869**	Armies of workers build the Transcontinental Railroad.
●	**1877**	Nez Perce War starts.
●	**1886**	Apache leader Geronimo surrenders to U.S. forces.
●	**1890**	death of Sitting Bull at Wounded Knee
●	**1897**	gold rush to the Yukon
●	**1899**	Nome, Alaska gold rush

How to Write A Journal Entry

People keep journals for many reasons. Some people record their hopes and dreams. Sometimes people want to keep a record of an important time or event, knowing that this will be useful in the future.

Journals are also a valuable primary source that can tell us a lot about how events occurred, how people lived, and about people's perspectives in the past.

Begin your journal entry.

Start with the date.

Write using the first person using the pronoun *I*.

Give details about what you did.

Describe your feelings about the event or situation.

Reread your diary entry and revise if necessary.

Imagine you are a prospector who has decided to go west in 1849. Be sure to answer these questions:

1. Where are you and when? Write the date plus the day of the week. (Future readers will want to know.)

2. How do you hear about the gold discovery? In the newspaper? From your neighbors? A letter from a friend or relative out West?

3. How do you get to the diggings — by steamboat? On horseback? What tools do you take?

4. Who are your companions, if any? (It could be your pet.)

5. What Indian tribes might you encounter?

6. Where do you go? Where and how do you live when you get there? In a mining camp? In a tent or in a cave? In an abandoned shack?

7. What do you have to eat?

8. If you strike gold, what will you do with your riches?

SAMPLE JOURNAL ENTRY

Sunday, April 3, 1849

I finally reached Sutter's Mill on Tuesday. It was a three-month journey aboard the ship and I was glad to see it end when we made port in San Francisco.

I didn't take any time to rest. I bought my supplies and headed by horse and wagon with a group of prospectors. This gold-digging is dirty business. There are rows and rows of tents as far as the eye can see and little dry ground with so many slop buckets along the tent path. The living conditions are rougher than I imagined, but I know my work will pay off.

I have been panning five days straight, and have some gold dust to show for it. The streams are ice cold, and my hands and feet go numb quickly, but I push on. The summer months will warm the stream, I hope.

Sometimes I wonder if coming out here was really a good idea. But I know I will find my fortune. I try to remind myself that I am out here not only for me, but also for my family.